T0193981

BORN AGAIN

THE WATER BIRTH

KYLE WHERRY

WESTBOW
PRESS®
A DIVISION OF THOMAS NELSON
& ZONDERVAN

WestBow Press books may be ordered through booksellers or by contacting:

WestBow Press
A Division of Thomas Nelson & Zondervan
1663 Liberty Drive
Bloomington, IN 47403
www.westbowpress.com
1 (866) 928-1240

ISBN: 978-1-9736-2260-4 (sc)
ISBN: 978-1-9736-2261-1 (e)

Library of Congress Control Number: 2018903339

Print information available on the last page.

WestBow Press rev. date: 04/09/2018

DEDICATION

To my parents Virginia Eileen and Richard (Raymond) Paul Wherry; every thought of both of you inspires me.

Thanks, Mom and Dad, for always being wonderful.

Love,

Your Son

TABLE OF CONTENTS

Introduction ix
Born Again xi

A: Death; Repent 1
B: Burial; Born of Water 5
B. 1. Remission 5
B. 2. Obey 9
B. 3. Baptized 11
B. 4. Righteous 13
B. 5. Requirements 15
B. 6. Name 17
B. 7. Permission 21
B. 8. Call 23
B. 9. Urgency 25
B. 10. Representative 27
B. 11. Came 29
B. 12. Defection 31
B. 13. Recap 33
B. 14. Three 35

C: Resurrection; Born of the Spirit 39

C. 1. Promise 39

C. 2. Birth 43

Takeaway 45

Plea 47

Questions 49

INTRODUCTION

This book shows the Scriptural support from the New King James Bible, for the 3 part answer given in Acts 2:38, and for the 2 requirements needed to enter God's kingdom in John 3:5.

It also shows the definitions from the New Exhaustive Strong's Concordance, for a more clear understanding of key words when English did not support their true meaning.

WE MUST BE BORN AGAIN

> "Jesus answered and said to him, "Most assuredly, I say to you, unless one is born again, he cannot see the kingdom of God.""

> —John 3:3

Nicodemus wanted to understand, how one could be born again (John 3:4).

> "Jesus answered, "Most assuredly, I say to you, unless one is born of Water [1] and the Spirit, [2] he cannot enter the kingdom of God.""

> —John 3:5

In the original Greek, *hudor* means water from rain.

A: DEATH; REPENT

"Now when they heard this, they were cut to the heart, and said to Peter and the rest of the apostles, "Men and brethren, what shall we do?""

—Acts 2:37

A true believer's first answered question should be; "what shall we do?"

> *Then Peter said to them,*
> *[A—Repent* (death)]
> —Acts 2:38

In the original Greek, *metanoeo* means to think differently or afterwards, to reconsider. It also means to morally feel compunction; anxiety arising from awareness of guilt.

"Also He spoke this parable to some who trusted in themselves that they were righteous, [dead works] and despised others: "Two men went up to the temple to pray, one a Pharisee and the other a tax collector. The Pharisee stood and prayed thus with himself, 'God, I thank you that I am not like other men—extortioners, unjust, adulterers, or even as this tax collector. I fast twice a week; I give tithes of all that I possess.' And the tax collector, standing afar off, would not so much as raise his eyes to heaven, but beat his breast, saying, 'God, be merciful to me a sinner!' I tell you, this man went down to his house justified rather than the other; for everyone who exalts himself will be humbled, and he who humbles himself will be exalted.'"

—Luke 18:9–14

Unlike the Pharisees, the tax collector was bearing fruits worthy of repentance (Matthew 3:8). Bearing fruits is referencing a state of mind that stirs the emotions and can manifest itself in a physically visible manner.

"For godly sorrow produces repentance leading to salvation, not to be regretted; but the sorrow of the world produces death."

—2nd Corinthians 7:10

"Then He said to them, "Thus it is written, and thus it was necessary for the Christ to suffer and to rise from the dead the third day, and that [A] repentance and [B] remission [Greek *aphesis*, pardon] of sins should be preached in His name to all nations, beginning at Jerusalem.""

—Luke 24:46–47

How do we obtain remission of sins in His name?

B: BURIAL; BORN OF WATER

REMISSION 1

And let every one of you be
[B—Baptized (burial)] *in the name of*
Jesus Christ for the remission of sins
—Acts 2:38

"Or do you not know that as many of us as were baptized into Christ Jesus were baptized into His death? Therefore we were buried with Him through baptism into death, that just as Christ was raised from the dead by the glory of the Father, even so we also should walk in newness of life."

—Romans 6:3–4

"This is a faithful saying: For if we died with Him, we shall also live with Him … If we are faithless, [Greek *apisteo,* to be unbelieving] He remains faithful; [Greek *pistos*, trustworthy] He cannot deny Himself."

—2nd Timothy 2:11, 13

"Therefore, leaving the discussion of the elementary principles of Christ, let us go on to perfection, not laying again the foundation of [A] repentance from dead works [faith in self—Luke 18:9, 11–12, chapter A] and of faith toward God, of the [B] doctrine of baptisms, of [C] laying on of hands, of resurrection of the dead, and of eternal judgement."

—Hebrews 6:1–2

The doctrine of baptisms is one of the foundational principles of Christ:

"For no other foundation can anyone lay than that which is laid, which is Jesus Christ."

—1st Corinthians 3:11

Once the foundation of Jesus Christ is laid then even;

> "If anyone's work is burned, he will suffer loss; but he himself will be saved, yet so as through fire."

—1st Corinthians 3:15

B: BURIAL; BORN OF WATER

OBEY 2

"For the time has come for judgement to begin at the house of God; and if it begins with us first, what will be the end of those who do not obey the gospel of God?"

—1st Peter 4:17

"And to give you who are troubled rest with us when the Lord Jesus is revealed from heaven with His mighty angels, in flaming fire taking vengeance on those who do not [I] Know God, and on those who do not [II] obey the gospel of our Lord Jesus Christ."

—2nd Thessalonians 1:7–8

We *must* obey the gospel. What is the gospel?

> "Moreover, brethren, I declare to you the gospel which I preached to you, which also you received and in which you stand, by which also you are saved, if you hold fast that word which I preached to you—unless you believed in vain. For I delivered to you first of all that which I also received: that Christ died for our sins according to the Scriptures, and that He was buried, and that He rose again the third day according to the Scriptures."
>
> —1ˢᵗ Corinthians 15:1–4

The gospel is the (A) death, (B) burial, and (C) resurrection of Christ.

We can obey the death, burial, and resurrection of Christ (gospel) by being "buried with Him through baptism into His death" (Romans 6:4, Acts 2:38, chapters A, B. 1).

B: BURIAL; BORN OF WATER

BAPTIZED 3

> "And He said to them, "Go into all the world and preach the gospel to every creature. He who believes and is baptized will be saved; but he who does not believe will be condemned."

—Mark 16:15–16

Believing—having faith in the gospel of Christ—comes first. Baptism—obeying the gospel (Romans 6:4)—has to come second because it is required (John 3:5, Acts 2:38, 2nd Thessalonians 1:7–8) to have the work of that faith.

> "What does it profit, my brethren, if someone says he has faith but does not have works? [Greek *ergon*; an act or

> deed being specific to that faith] Can faith save him?"
>
> —James 2:14

The implication is that no, it can't.

> "You believe that there is one God. You do well. Even the demons believe— and tremble!"
>
> —James 2:19

> "But do you want to Know, O foolish man, that faith without works is dead?"
>
> —James 2:20

Abraham's, and Rahab's works [*ergon*] were a specific action to what they had faith in (James 2:21–26).

Works of faith in the gospel of Christ (Romans 6:4) guarantee saving faith (James 2:14).

B: BURIAL; BORN OF WATER

RIGHTEOUS 4

> "As it is written: "There is none righteous, no, not one.""
>
> —Romans 3:10

Works of righteousness guarantee access to God's kingdom.

> "Not by works of righteousness which we have done, but according to His mercy He saved us, through the washing [Greek *loutron*, baptism] of regeneration, [Greek *paliggenesia*, rebirth] and renewing of the Holy Spirit."
>
> —Titus 3:5

According to God's Word, Jesus saves us through baptism, which is not a work of righteousness but a water rebirth (John 3:3, 5).

> "For by grace you have been saved through faith, and that not of yourselves; it is the gift of God, not of works, lest anyone should boast."
>
> —Ephesians 2:8–9

By faith we believe, by faith we repent, by faith we are buried with Christ through baptism into His Death (Romans 6:3–4, chapter B. 1), and by faith we receive the Holy Spirit.

> "And such were some of you. But you were washed, but you were sanctified, [Greek *hagiazo*, made holy, purified] but you were Justified [Greek *dikaioo*, to render, just, or innocent; free, *righteous*] in the name of the Lord Jesus [Acts 2:38(B)] and by the Spirit [Acts 2:38(C)] of our God."
>
> —1st Corinthians 6:11

B: BURIAL; BORN OF WATER

REQUIREMENTS 5

The born-again dispensation of grace could not begin until after Jesus ascended and was glorified (John 7:39) with the glory He had with the Father before the world was created (John 17:5). Only then could we be born of the Spirit of the born-again births. (John 3:5).

This is why the prophets (Abraham et al.) and those who died having faith in the promises of God had to go to Abraham's bosom (Greek *kolpos*, bay; bosom, creek) in Sheol and wait.

Hence, when Jesus told the thief on the cross who had faith in Jesus's promise of His kingdom, "Today you will be with Me in paradise" [Greek *paradeisos*, an Eden] (Luke 23:43), He was referring to the believer's district (Abraham's bosom) in Sheol (Greek *shehole*; the world of the dead where the rich man was tormented in hell, and where Lazarus was comforted with water: Luke 16:22–25).

This is where Jesus was ministering until His resurrection (1st Peter 3:19–20). God's Word tells us after Jesus was resurrected;

> "Jesus said to her, "Do not cling to Me, for I have not yet ascended to My Father; but go to My brethren and say to them, 'I am ascending to My Father and your Father, and to My God and your God.'""

> —John 20:17

> "(Now this, "He ascended"—what does it mean but that He also first descended into the lower parts of the earth? He who descended is also the One who ascended far above all the heavens, that He might fill all things.)"

> —Ephesians 4:9–10

Only after Jesus ascended to the Father and was glorified were all on earth and all in Abraham's bosom—paradise—able to be born of water and the Spirit, which are the requirements (John 3:5) for entering God's kingdom.

B: BURIAL; BORN OF WATER

NAME 6

> "And Jesus came and spoke to them, saying, "All authority has been given to Me in heaven and on earth. Go therefore and make disciples of all the nations, baptizing them in the Name of the Father and of the Son and of the Holy Spirit.""
>
> —Matthew 28:18–19

After Jesus ascended and was glorified, every time the apostles baptized, they did so in the name of the Lord Jesus Christ because they understood the name (singular) of the Father, Son, and the Holy Spirit is Jesus.

Peter commanded the Gentiles, who had already received the Holy Spirit (born of the Spirit; John 3:5) to be baptized (Acts 2:38) in the name of the Lord (Acts 10:44–48).

> "There is one body and one Spirit, just as you were called in one hope of your calling; one Lord, [Greek *Kurios*; supreme in authority] one faith, one baptism."

> —Ephesians 4:4–5

Paul found disciples who were believers baptized by John the Baptist, and they were baptized again but that time in the name of the Lord Jesus (Acts 19:1–5).

John's baptism of repentance was not sufficient for salvation to the unrighteous, because only baptism in the name of Jesus Christ is required for salvation (Acts 2:38).

> "Nor is there salvation in any other, for there is no other name under heaven given among men by which we must be saved."

> —Acts 4:12

> "For there are three that bear witness in heaven: The Father, [God] the

Word, [Son; John 1:14] and the Holy Spirit; and these three are one." [Jesus]

—1st John 5:7

"For in Him [Christ Jesus] dwells all the fullness of the Godhead bodily; and you are complete in Him, who is the head of all principality and power."

—Colossians 2:9–10

"And the Lord shall be King over all the earth. In that day it shall be—"The Lord [Hebrew *Yhovah*, God] is one," And His name one."

—Zechariah 14:9

B: BURIAL; BORN OF WATER

PERMISSION 7

"These things I have written to you who believe in the name of the Son of God, that you may know that you have eternal life, and that you may continue to believe in the name of the Son of God."

—1ˢᵗ John 5:13

"And this is the will of Him who sent Me, that everyone who sees the Son and believes in Him may have everlasting life; and I will raise him up at the last day."

—John 6:40

"But these are written that you may believe that Jesus is the Christ, the Son of God, and that believing you may have life in His name."

—John 20:31

After believing, how can we have life in His name?

B: BURIAL; BORN OF WATER

CALL 8

"For with the heart one believes unto righteousness, and with the mouth confession is made unto salvation. For the Scripture says, "Whoever believes on Him will not be put to shame." For there is no distinction between Jew and Greek, for the same Lord over all is rich to all who call upon Him. For "whoever calls on the name of the Lord shall be saved." How then shall they call on Him in whom they have not believed? And how shall they believe in Him of whom they have not heard? And how shall they hear without a preacher?"

—Romans 10:10–14

Now we see that to believe is not the end to salvation, but the first decision an individual must make, that should lead to *call* on the name of the Lord for salvation.

> "And it shall come to pass that whoever calls on the name of the Lord shall be saved."

> —Acts 2:21

How do we *call* on the name of the Lord for salvation?

> "Then he said, 'The God of our fathers has chosen you that you should know His will, and see the Just One, and hear the voice of His mouth. For you will be His witness to all men of what you have seen and heard. And now why are you waiting? Arise and be baptized, and wash away your sins, calling on the name of the Lord.'"

> —Acts 22:14–16

B: BURIAL; BORN OF WATER

URGENCY 9

After Philip preached Jesus to the eunuch, as soon as he saw water he wanted to be baptized.
(Acts 8:35–36)

The urgency comes from what is required to enter God's kingdom (John 3:5).

> "Then Phillip said, "If you believe with all your heart, you may." And he answered and said, "I believe that Jesus Christ is the Son of God.""
>
> —Acts 8:37
>
> "So he commanded the chariot to stand still. And both Phillip and the

Eunuch went down into the water, and he baptized him."

—Acts 8:38

"Now when they came up out of the water, the Spirit of the Lord caught Phillip away, so that the eunuch saw him no more; and he went on his way rejoicing."

—Acts 8:39

The eunuch was made a disciple (Matthew 28:19, chapter B. 6); he was in God's Word, he confessed that he believed that Jesus Christ was the Son of God; and was baptized (obeying the gospel, 2nd Thessalonians 1:7–8, chapter B. 2).

"So they said, "believe on the Lord Jesus Christ, and you will be saved, you and your household.""

—Acts 16:31

Immediately at midnight the Philippian jailer and all his family were baptized (Acts 16:33).

B: BURIAL; BORN OF WATER

REPRESENTATIVE 10

"How much more shall the blood of Christ, who through the Eternal Spirit offered Himself without spot to God, cleanse your conscience from dead works [faith in self—Luke 18:9, 11–12, chapter A] to serve the living God?"

—Hebrews 9:14

How do you cleanse your conscience?

"There is also an antitype [Greek *antitupon*, a representative] which now saves us—baptism (not the removal of the filth of the flesh, [blood] but the answer of a good conscience toward God [water]), through the resurrection of Jesus Christ."

—1ˢᵗ Peter 3:21

"Let us draw near with a true heart in full assurance of faith, having our hearts sprinkled from an evil conscience and our bodies washed with pure water." [Greek *hudor,* rain]

—Hebrews 10:22

B: BURIAL; BORN OF WATER

CAME 11

"It came to pass in those days that Jesus came from Nazareth of Galilee, and was baptized [Greek *baptizo*, immersed, submerged, made fully wet] by John in the Jordan."

—Mark 1:9

Jesus was baptized with water unto repentance (Matthew 3:11); for the sins of the world.

"This is He who came by water [Greek *hudor*, rain] and blood—Jesus Christ; not only by water, but by water and blood. And it is the Spirit who bears witness, because the Spirit is truth."

—1st John 5:6

"But I have a baptism to be baptized with, and how distressed I am till it is accomplished!" [Blood sacrifice]

—Luke 12:50

Born of water (John 3:5, Titus 3:5, chapter B. 4), baptism, and came have the same meaning.

B: BURIAL; BORN OF WATER

DEFECTION 12

"That we should no longer be children, tossed to and fro and carried about with every wind of doctrine, by the trickery of men, in the cunning craftiness of deceitful plotting."

—Ephesians 4:14

"Let no one deceive you by any means; for that day [the second coming of Christ] will not come unless the falling away [Greek *apostasia*, defection from truth] comes first, and the man of sin is revealed, the son of perdition."

—2nd Thessalonians 2:3

"Now the Spirit expressly says that in latter times some will depart from the faith, giving heed to deceiving spirits and doctrines of demons."

—1ˢᵗ Timothy 4:1

"For the time will come when they will not endure sound doctrine, [Hebrews 6:2, chapter B. 1] but according to their own desires, because they have itching ears, they will heap up for themselves teachers; and they will turn their ears away from the truth, and be turned aside to fables."

—2ⁿᵈ Timothy 4:3–4

B: BURIAL; BORN OF WATER

RECAP 13

God's Word says:	*Baptism is not necessary for salvation says:*
Unless one is reborn of water from rain and the Spirit, he cannot enter the kingdom of God (John 3:3, 5).	You need only a natural birth and a rebirth of the Holy Spirit to enter God's kingdom.
Be baptized in the name of Jesus for the forgiveness of sins (Acts 2:38).	You don't need baptism for the forgiveness of sins.

God's Word says:	Baptism is not necessary for salvation says:
Jesus saves us through baptism, it's not a work of righteousness, and it is a water rebirth (Titus 3:5).	Jesus saves us without baptism because it would be considered a work of righteousness, and it is not a water rebirth.
Be baptized, and wash away your sins (Acts 22:16).	Baptism doesn't wash away sins.
There is a representative which now saves us— baptism (1st Peter 3:21).	Baptism doesn't save us.
Sound doctrine (Hebrews 6:2).	Fable (2nd Timothy 4:4).

B: BURIAL; BORN OF WATER

THREE 14

Through the eternal Spirit
—Hebrews 9:14

Jesus came by water from rain (Mark 1:9) and blood (Luke 12:50), so we could obey the gospel (2nd Thessalonians 1:7–8) and be born again (John 3:3) of water from rain and the Spirit (John 3:5).

> "And there are three that bear witness on earth: the Spirit, [Acts 2:38(C)] the water, [Acts 2:38(B)] and the blood; [1st Peter 1:18–19] and these three agree as one."
>
> —1st John 5:8

"Jesus answered and said to him, "Are you the teacher of Israel, and do not know these things?""

—John *3:10*

"For the law, having a shadow of the good [gospel—1ˢᵗ Corinthians 15:1–4, chapter B. 2] things to come, and not the very image of the things, can never with these same sacrifices, which they offer continually year by year, make those who approach perfect."

—Hebrews 10:1

"When they go into the tabernacle of meeting, or when they come near the altar to minister, to burn an offering made by fire to the Lord, [blood sacrifice] they shall wash with water, lest they die.

—Exodus 30:20

Nicodemus should have understood better than anyone that being born again (John 3:3) meant born of water and the Spirit (John 3:5). Teaching God's law and performing the rituals continually were shadows of the salvation to come, which involved a blood sacrifice and the washing of water to enter the presence of the Holy Spirit.

C: RESURRECTION; BORN OF THE SPIRIT

PROMISE 1

And you shall receive the gift of the
*[C—Holy Spirit (*resurrection)]*
—Acts 2:38

"For the promise is to you and to your children, and to all who are afar off, as many as the Lord our God will call,"

—Acts 2:39

"And being assembled together with them, He commanded them not to depart from Jerusalem, but to wait for the Promise of the Father, "which," He said, "you have heard from Me; for John truly baptized with water, but

you shall be baptized with the Holy
Spirit not many days from now.""

—Acts 1:4–5

"Then I remembered the word of
the Lord, how He said, 'John indeed
baptized [*baptizo*; fully immersed] you
with water, but you shall be Baptized
[*baptizo*; fully immersed] with the
Holy Spirit.'"

—Acts 11:16

"If you love Me, keep My
commandments. And I [Jesus] will
pray the Father, and He will give you
another Helper, that He may abide with
you forever—the Spirit of truth**,** whom
the world cannot receive, because it
neither sees Him nor knows Him; but
you know Him, for He dwells with you
and will be in you. I will not leave you
orphans; I will come to you."

—John 14:15–18

"Nevertheless I tell you the truth. It is
to your advantage that I go away; for

if I do not go away, the Helper will not come to you; but if I depart, I will send Him to you. And when He has come, He will convict the world of sin, and of righteousness, and of judgement: of sin, because they do not believe in Me; of righteousness, because I go to my Father and you see Me no more; of Judgement, because the ruler of this world is judged. "I still have many things to say to you, but you cannot bear them now. However, when He, the Spirit of truth, has come, He will guide you into all truth; for he will not speak on His own authority, but whatever He hears He will speak; and He will tell you things to come. He will glorify Me, for He will take of what is Mine and declare it to you. All things that the Father has are Mine. Therefore I said that He will take of Mine and declare it to you."

—John 16:7–15

"Then you shall know that I am in the midst of Israel: I am the Lord your God and there is no other. My people shall never be put to shame. "And it shall come to pass afterward That I will pour out My Spirit on all flesh; Your sons and your daughters shall prophesy, Your old men shall dream dreams, Your young men shall see visions. And also on My menservants and on My maidservants I will pour out My Spirit in those days."

Joel 2:27–29

"If you then, being evil, know how to give good gifts to your children, how much more will your heavenly Father give the Holy Spirit to those who ask Him!"

—Luke 11:13

— "John answered, saying to all, "I indeed baptize you with water; but One mightier than I is coming, whose sandal strap I am not worthy to loose. [Jesus] He will baptize you with the Holy Spirit and fire.""

—Luke 3:16

C: RESURRECTION BORN OF THE SPIRIT

BIRTH 2

"Then there appeared to them divided tongues, as of fire, and one sat upon each of them. And they were all filled with the Holy Spirit and began to speak with other tongues, as the Spirit gave them utterance."

Acts 2:3–4

"Now when the apostles who were at Jerusalem heard that Samaria had received the word of God, they sent Peter and John to them, who, when they had come down, prayed for them that they might receive the Holy Spirit. For as yet He had fallen upon none of them. They had only been baptized in the name of the Lord Jesus. Then they laid hands on them, and they received the Holy Spirit."

Acts 8:14–17

"And Ananias went his way and entered the house; and laying his hands on him he said, "Brother Saul, the Lord Jesus, who appeared to you on the road as you came, has sent me that you may receive your sight and be filled with the Holy Spirit.""

Acts 9:17

"And as I began to speak, the Holy Spirit fell upon them, as upon us at the beginning."

—Acts 11:15

"And when Paul had laid hands on them, the Holy Spirit came upon them, and they spoke with tongues and prophesied. Now the men were about twelve in all."

Acts 19:6–7

TAKEAWAY

Here is *Born Again* in a nutshell: unless you are baptized in the name of the Lord Jesus Christ and you shall receive the gift of the Holy Spirit, you cannot enter the kingdom of God (John 3:5 [1, 2]; Acts 2:38 [A, B, C]).

We must I) know God, and II) obey the gospel: — Baptism in the name of Jesus (2nd Thessalonians 1:7–8, chapter B. 2).

With (A) repentance and (B) remission of sins; — baptism in the name of Jesus (Luke 24:47, chapters A, B. 1), we are born again—John 3:3 of 1) water from rain; —baptism in the name of Jesus (John 3:5, chapter B. 4), and you shall receive the gift of the (C) Holy Spirit (Acts 2:38).

PLEA

"But, speaking the truth in love, may grow up in all things into Him who is the head—Christ—from whom the whole body, joined and knit together by what every joint supplies, according to the effective working by which every part does its share, causes growth of the body for the edifying of itself in love."

—Ephesians 4:15–16

My hope is that you put God's Word above humanity's opinion of it, and teach your family and friends what is required to enter the kingdom of God from the minute you believe. That way, the doctrine of baptisms will be the first thing they understand.

In Jesus (John 15:1–8),
Kyle Wherry

QUESTIONS

What are the born again births?

A.   What does repent mean?

B1   How do we obtain pardon for sins?

B2   What is the gospel, and how do we obey it?

B3   What must come after believing and why?

B4   How are we made righteous?

B5   What are the requirements?

B6   What is the name of the Father, Son, and Holy Spirit?

B7   Believing gives us permission to have what?

B8   How are we to call on the name of Jesus for salvation?

B9   What is the urgency?

B10   How can we cleanse our consciences?

B11   What does the word *came* mean?

B12   When approximately will the defection from truth happen?

B13   What is the recap?

B14   What are the three on earth who bear witness?

C1   Will we receive the Holy Spirit?

C2   What does the Spirit birth look like?

What is the takeaway?

What is my reason?

SCRIPTURE BY CHAPTER

Born Again — John 3:3–5

A. Death — Acts 2:37–38, Luke 18:9–14, 24:46–47, Matthew 3:8, 2nd Corinthians 7:10

B.1. Remission — Acts 2:38, Romans 6:3–4, 2nd Timothy 2:11, 13, Hebrews 6:1–2, 1st Corinthians 3:11, 15, Luke 18:11–12

B. 2. Obey — 1st Peter 4:17, 2nd Thessalonians 1:7-8, 1st Corinthians 15:1–4, Romans 6:4, Acts 2:38

B. 3. Baptized — Mark 16:15–16, Romans 6:4, John 3:5, Acts 2:38, 2nd Thessalonians 1:7-8, James 2:14, 19–26

B. 4. Righteous — Romans 3:10, Titus 3:5, John 3:3, 5, Ephesians 2:8–9, Romans 6:3–4, Acts 2:38, 1st Corinthians 6:11

B. 5. Requirements — John 3:5, 7:39, 20:17, 17:5, Luke 16:22–25, 23:43, 1st Peter 3:19–20, Ephesians 4:9–10

B. 6. Name — Matthew 28:18–19, John 3:5, Acts 2:38, 4:12, 10:44–48, 19:1–5, Ephesians 4:4–5, John 1:14, 1st John 5:7, Colossians 2:9–10, Zechariah 14:9

B. 7. Permission — 1st John 5:13, John 6:40, 20:31

B. 8. Call — Romans 10:10–14, Acts 2:21, 22:14–16

B. 9. Urgency — Acts 8:35–39, 16:31, 33, John 3:5, Matthew 28:19, 2nd Thessalonians 1:7–8

B. 10. Representative — Hebrews 9:14, 10:22, Luke 18:9, 11–12, 1st Peter 3:21

B. 11. Came — Mark 1:9, Matthew 3:11, 1st John 5:6, Luke 12:50, John 3:5, Titus 3:5

B. 12. Defection — Ephesians 4:14, 2nd Thessalonians 2:3, 1st Timothy 4:1, 2nd Timothy 4:3–4

B.13. Recap — John 3:3, 5, Acts 2:38, Titus 3:5, Acts 22:16, 1st Peter 3:21, Hebrews 6:2, 2nd Timothy 4:4

B.14. Three — Hebrews 9:14, 10:1 Mark 1:9, Luke 12:50, 2nd Thessalonians 1:7-8, John 3:3, 5, 10, Acts 2:38, 1st Peter 1:18–19, 1st John 5:8, 1st Corinthians 15:1–4, Exodus 30:20,

C.1. Promise — Acts 1:4–5, 2:38–39, 11:16, Joel 2:27–29, John 14:15–18, 16:7–15, Luke 3:16, 11:13

C.2. Birth — Acts 2:3–4, 8:14–17, 9:17, 11:15, 19:6–7

Takeaway — John 3:3, 5, Acts 2:38, 2nd Thessalonians 1:7–8, Luke 24:47

Plea — Ephesians 4:15–16, John 15:1–8

SCRIPTURE

Exodus 3:20

Joel 2:27–29

Zechariah 14:9

Matthew 3:8, 11, 28:18–19

Mark 1:9, 16:15–16

Luke 3:16, 11:9–13, 12:50, 16:22–25, 18:9–14, 23:43, 24:46–47,

John 1:14, 3:3–5, 10, 6:40, 7:39, 14:15–18, 15:1–8, 16:7–15, 17:5, 20:17, 31

Acts 1:4–5, 2: 3–4, 21, 28–29, 36–39, 4:12, 8:14–17, 8:35–39, 10:44–48, 11:15–16, 14:17, 16:31–33, 19:1–7, 22:14–16

Romans 3:10, 6:3–4, 10, 10:10–14

1ˢᵗ Corinthians 3:11, 15, 6:11, 15:1–4

2ⁿᵈ Corinthians 7:10

Ephesians 2:8–9, 4:4–5, 9–10, 14–16

Colossians 2:9–10

2ⁿᵈ Thessalonians 1:7–8, 2:3

1ˢᵗ Timothy 4:1

2ⁿᵈ Timothy 2:11, 13, 4:3–4

Titus 3:5

Hebrews 6:1–2, 9:14, 10:1, 22

James 2:14, 19–26

1ˢᵗ Peter 1:18–19, 3:19–21, 4:17

1ˢᵗ John 5:6–8, 13

ABOUT THE AUTHOR

As a longtime student of Bible prophecy, I discovered that to get the clearest understanding, I had to refrain from adding assumptions, opinions, or theories and simply let God's Word explain itself. When I applied this method to the teachings on born again, born of water, baptism, and what is required to enter God's kingdom, I discovered a more clear understanding on this topic as well.

My hope is that through this study, you will understand this topic better and have a better way of studying the Bible as a whole, which will help you to know God and share His truth.

Printed in the United States
By Bookmasters